Courageous Generosity
for teens

A Bible Study on Selflessness for Young Women

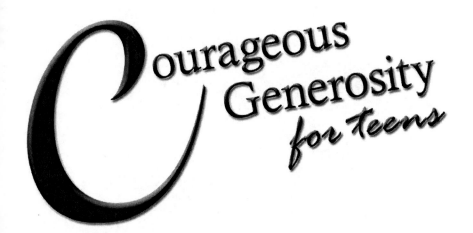

Courageous Generosity for Teens

A Bible Study on Selflessness for Young Women
by Stacy Mitch with Emily Stimpson

EMMAUS
ROAD
PUBLISHING

Steubenville, Ohio
www.emmausroad.org

Emmaus Road Publishing
601 Granard Parkway
Steubenville, Ohio 43952

Library of Congress Control Number: 2015938386
ISBN: 978-1-941447-26-0

Cover design by Valerie Pokorny
Layout design by Mairead Cameron

CONTENTS

Introduction

God wants to make you a deal.

Here's what He's offering: love, peace, and happiness.

But, not just any old love, peace, and happiness.

He's offering His love—a love that never falters and never fails, a love more lasting and more real than any love you've ever known, and a love so passionate that it will stop at nothing to win and keep your heart.

He's also offering you His peace—a peace that withstands every trial this crazy, mixed-up world can throw at you, a peace that answers questions, stills doubt, and clears up confusion, a peace that comforts, consoles, and protects.

And He's offering you His happiness—a happiness that doesn't change with the seasons, a happiness that no enemy, no matter how powerful, can take from you, a happiness that lasts and lasts and lasts, pure, undiluted joy for all eternity.

Basically, He's offering to make you not just His creation, but His daughter, giving you a glory greater than that of any angel.

That's what He's offering. But what is He asking in return?

One thing: For you to love like He loves.

God wants you to love Him, your family, your friends, your classmates, your teachers, your neighbors, and absolute strangers with the undying, unwavering, all merciful love of an all-knowing, all-powerful God of the Universe.

Easy, right?

On one level, yes, it is easy. Not because you or anyone else is even remotely capable of that kind of love. You're not. Rather, it's easy because He is. God takes the love that He possesses and pours it into your heart. Your job is just to accept it and pass it on.

There is, however, one catch. Because human hearts are so little and weak, accepting that love hurts. So does giving it away. When you love like God loves, you suffer. You suffer because both the receiving and giving of His love requires you to battle your own selfishness and self-will. And that means making sacrifices, painful sacrifices. It means practicing courageous generosity.

That's what loving like God loves ultimately requires: courageous generosity. What courageous generosity looks like in practice is what this study is all about. And your assignment, when the study is over and done with, is to answer one question: Are you ready to make a deal?

Courageous Generosity

"It's not all about me."

Those five words are easy to say, but hard to believe. Really hard. After all, the culture tells you from sun up to sun down that it actually is "all about you." The music you listen to, the movies you watch, the advertisements you see, even the technology you use, all encourage you to think about yourself before you think of others.

It sounds harsh, but it's true.

The tech industry, the entertainment industry, and the advertising industry are all out to convince you that your own happiness should come first, that you should buy what you want, say what you want, and do what you want, even if it means somebody else gets hurt. The reason they want to convince you of that? They're out to make a profit and encouraging selfishness is the surest way to do that.

Don't be taken in by their lies. Look instead to Jesus, who encourages something entirely different. At the Last Supper, He washed the feet of the Apostles, a job that only the lowliest of servants would do. In doing that, He called His followers to serve all men and women, just as He, the God of the universe, serves us. He called us to put others first, to give everything, even our lives, for another's good.

That's a radical call. And it takes courage to answer it. It takes courage to be generous when everything and everyone around you encourages just the opposite. It takes courage to tell the culture that you're not buying what it's selling.

But, here's the good news. God never calls you to anything without also giving you the grace to answer the call. He'll give you all the grace you need to practice courageous generosity. You just have to ask. It also, of course, helps to understand what you're asking for.

COURAGE

Read

1. In Joshua 1:1–9, what does God ask Joshua to do? Why, according to Numbers 13:25–33, will that require courage?

_____

_____

_____

2. To help Joshua face those obstacles and his own fears, what promise does God make to Joshua in Joshua 1:5?

_____

_____

3. Describe what happens in Exodus 14:10–14. What do the Israelites say they prefer? What causes them to say that?

_____

_____

_____

4. Read Matthew 26:47, 56 and 26:69–75. What did the Apostles do to Jesus? Why did they do that?

_____

_____

_____

_____

5. What reason does Jesus give you in Matthew 10:29–31 to not be afraid?

_____

_____

6. According to Romans 8:14–17, what has God given to you that will prevent you from becoming a slave to your fears? How does God help you be courageous?

_____

_____

_____

Reflect

1. Has the Lord ever asked you, like Joshua, to take on a challenge that seemed impossible? How did you react at first? Were you afraid? If so, did you conquer your fear? How? What did God do to help you?

_____

_____

_____

_____

2. The Israelites almost let their fears enslave them. Have you ever been a slave to your fears, afraid to do something or let go of something because you were afraid of what might happen if you did? Describe the situation. What are some other fears that might enslave us?

_____

_____

_____

3. The Apostles were afraid to admit they were Jesus' followers. Why? Does the same thing happen to Christians in today's culture? Why might someone deny believing in Christ or believing what the Church teaches? Have you ever felt tempted to do that? Explain. How did you deal with the temptation?

_____

_____

_____

GENEROSITY

Read

1. Read the following passages. According to each passage, what are you required to do? How do those actions demonstrate generosity?

a) Romans 12:10–21; 15:1–3 _____

_____

b) Ephesians 4:1–3 _____

_____

c) 1 Thessalonians 5:13–15 _____

_____

d) 1 Timothy 6:18 _____

_____

2. According to Proverbs 11:25 and Proverbs 22:9, what happens to you when you are generous?

_____

_____

3. Think about Christ's life. Can you name at least three ways He practiced courageous generosity?

_____

_____

_____

Reflect

1. Who is the most generous person you know? Describe them. What do they do that shows generosity? Why do you think they do that? How do they affect other people?

_____

_____

_____

_____

_____

_____

2. What is the most generous thing anyone has ever done for you? Describe what happened. How did that make you feel? What did you do in response? Has that helped you become more generous to others? Why or why not?

_____

_____

_____

3. Is there anything in particular with which you struggle to be generous? Clothes? Money? Your time? Sympathy? Something else? What is the hardest thing for you to give? Why do you think that is? What are some practical steps you can take to make generosity a habit?

_____

_____

_____

Respond

1. Be grateful for the generosity of others. Make it a habit not only to say thank you for what people do for you and give to you, but also write them a little "thank you" note to let them know how much you appreciate their efforts.

2. Don't be afraid to speak up and courageously defend Christ and the Church when someone attacks them in conversation or in the classroom.

3. Ask God every day in prayer to show you the people in your life who are in need of your generosity and for the grace to help give them what they need.

MEMORY VERSE

"I will not fail you
or forsake you . . . Only be strong
and very courageous."
Joshua 1:5b, 7a

GRACE IN ACTION

What does courageous generosity look like in action? For an example, we don't have to look any further than Mother Teresa (now officially known as Blessed Teresa of Calcutta).

Mother Teresa lived for others. In the slums of Calcutta, she begged for the poor. She also fed the poor, clothed the poor, and lavished her love on the sick, the deformed, and the dying— holding in her arms the men, women, and children who no one else would touch. She defended the right to life of the littlest and weakest among us, and she did it all while owning nothing herself, giving every gift she received to those most desperately in need. In her own convent, she even took the worst room for herself, the room next to the latrines, and took on the worst chore: cleaning the latrines.

You can't get any more generous than that.

BY THE BOOK

Here's what the Catechism of the Catholic Church has to say about courage and generosity.

COURAGE: "The moral virtue that ensures firmness in difficulties and constancy in the pursuit of the good. It strengthens the resolve to resist temptations and to overcome obstacles in the moral life. . . . [Courage] enables one to conquer fear, even fear of death, and to face trials and persecutions. It disposes one even to renounce and sacrifice his life in defense of a just cause" (1808).

GENEROSITY: "On coming into the world, man is not equipped with everything he needs for developing his bodily and spiritual life. He needs others. Differences appear tied to age, physical abilities, intellectual or moral aptitudes, the benefits derived from social commerce, and the distribution of wealth [Cf. GS 29 § 2]. . . . These differences belong to God's plan, who wills that each receive what he needs from others, and that those endowed with particular 'talents' share the benefits with those who need them" (1936–1937).

"The principal act of courage is to endure and withstand dangers doggedly rather than to attack them."

St. Thomas Aquinas

"It takes courage to tell the culture you're not buying what it's selling."

Sacrifice: The Way to Joy

God wants you to have it all. He wants you to have all the love, all the joy, and all the peace He has to give. But in order to have it all, you have to be willing not to have it all.

In other words, before you can say yes to all God has to give, you have to learn to say no to some of what the world has to give. You have to learn to deny your own will, and choose God's will. You have to learn to put others' needs before your own. You have to learn to accept suffering without complaint.

And the way you learn that is through sacrifice.

That's not, of course, what the culture says. The culture likes to pretend that sacrifice isn't necessary, that happiness can be had American Idol style—instantly, without working, waiting, or making compromises.

But American Idol isn't the real world. In the real world, good things come at a cost. And eternal joy is no exception.

Read

1. Read Genesis 3:21. What does God sacrifice in this passage? What does that sacrifice literally accomplish? What does it

figuratively accomplish? What does that tell you about the relationship between sacrifice and sin?

_____

_____

_____

_____

2. What other reason is there for sacrifice according to Genesis 8:13–22? What specific reason does Noah have to make that kind of sacrifice in this passage?

_____

_____

_____

3. Read Genesis 17:16–19 and 1 Samuel 1:9–19. Then answer the following questions.

a) What does God promise to both Abraham and Hannah?

_____

_____

_____

b) What does God then ask of Abraham in Genesis 22:1–2? What does Hannah promise God she will do in 1 Samuel 1:11?

_____

_____

_____

_____

c) According to James 2:21–23, what did God really want of Abraham?

_____

_____

_____

d) Why was Hannah willing to make such a sacrifice?

_____

_____

4. Although the ancient Israelites made lots of sacrifices, God wasn't always pleased with those sacrifices. According to the passages below, with what types of sacrifices is God not pleased? With what sacrifices is He pleased?

	Displeasing Sacrifices	Pleasing Sacrifices
Amos 5:21–24		
Malachi 1:6–9		
Hebrews 11:4		

5. If God wasn't after blood, what was the point of asking Israel to make all those animal sacrifices? (See Hebrews 10:1–5)

_____

_____

_____

_____

6. According to Hebrews 10:12–18, what is the one sacrifice that truly atones for sins?

_____

_____

7. Christ's sacrifice on the Cross has made it possible for you to spend eternal life with God. So why, according to the following passages, should you continue to make sacrifices? What do your sacrifices obtain for you and others?

a) Colossians 1:24 _____

_____

b) Romans 5:1–5 _____

_____

c) Philippians 1:29 _____

_____

8. According to Romans 12:1, how are you to worship God?

_____

_____

Reflect

1. Have you ever made a sacrifice as a way of saying you were sorry for something you had done? Describe what happened and what you did.

_____

_____

2. Think about your response to God when He answers your prayers and delivers you from a difficult situation. Have you ever made a spiritual sacrifice in thanks? If not, what is a spiritual sacrifice you can make the next time a prayer is answered? How do you think this will change the way you feel about God's response to your prayers?

_____

_____

_____

_____

3. Have you ever been asked, as Abraham and Hannah were, to sacrifice something that was very important to you? How did you respond? Why did you respond that way? How will you try to respond the next time you're asked to give up something precious?

_____

_____

_____

4. Have you ever made a sacrifice with the wrong attitude? Describe the situation. How did you feel afterwards? What were the consequences?

_____

_____

5. What do you think it means to offer your body as a "living sacrifice"? List the different ways that God might ask you to do that.

_____

_____

_____

6. Is there any sacrifice God is asking you to make right now that you haven't been willing to make? If so, what has been stopping you? What do you think will happen when you make that sacrifice? What action do you need to take in order to do what God is asking?

_____

_____

_____

Respond

1. Make a spiritual sacrifice. Pray an extra Our Father, Hail Mary, and Glory Be every day for one special prayer intention.

2. Make a corporal (physical) sacrifice. Every Friday, give up some special treat (sweets, Frappuccinos, or meat) and offer the sacrifice for a prayer intention.

3. Make an emotional sacrifice. The next time someone says something mean to you or insults you, bite your tongue and walk away without defending yourself.

MEMORY VERSE

"I appeal to you therefore, brethren,
by the mercies of God, to present your bodies
as a living sacrifice, holy and acceptable to God,
which is your spiritual worship."
Romans 12:1

GOD LOVES A CHEERFUL GIVER

That may be one of the most over-used clichés of all time. But it's true. God does love a cheerful giver.

A sacrifice is only as good as the attitude with which it is made. Sacrifices made grudgingly or resentfully don't add much to the treasury of saints. They also don't do much for the giver's soul.

When you make a sacrifice, big or small, material or spiritual, don't grumble or complain. Also, don't remind people of it again and again. The only thing worse than a grumpy giver is a giver who never lets others forget what's been given.

Basically, when making sacrifices, the same rules apply as when fasting: "Do not look dismal, like the hypocrites, for they disfigure their faces so that their fasting may be seen by men. Truly, I say to you, they have their reward. But when you fast, anoint your head and wash your face, that your fasting may not be seen by men but by your Father who is in secret; and your Father who sees in secret will reward you" (Mt 6:16–18).

"IT'S THE LITTLE THINGS THAT COUNT"

In days gone by, some people suffered from the misapprehension that only grand, glorious, and gigantic sacrifices counted, that is, fasting for forty days and forty nights, sitting atop a pillar for twenty years, or wearing the latest in hair shirts. But St. Thérèse of Lisieux, with her Little Way, reminded the world that little sacrifices matter too, that in fact, they often matter more.

That's because all the hair shirts in the world aren't worth much if you can't make the little sacrifices charity demands: holding your tongue, turning the other cheek, or listening to another's problems rather than talking about your own.

Not only does charity demand little spiritual and corporal sacrifices, so does your station in life. Most teenagers (or most people for that matter) aren't called to sit on top of pillars. You're called to obey your parents, help your friends, and be nice to the kids at school that nobody else is nice to.

The sacrifices God wants you to make are usually found in the daily grind of life. They are rarely great and even more rarely exotic. Eating soggy Brussels sprouts without complaining is unlikely to come up in canonization proceedings. Nonetheless, sacrifices such as those pave the road to sainthood.

> "But what does it all mean?" asked Susan when they were somewhat calmer.
>
> "It means," said Aslan, "that though the witch knew the Deep Magic, there is a magic deeper still which she did not know. Her knowledge goes back only to the dawn of Time. But if she could have looked a little further back, into the stillness and the darkness before Time dawned, she would have read there a different incantation. She would have known that when a willing victim who had committed no treachery was killed in a traitor's stead, the Table would crack and Death itself would start working backward."
>
> C.S. Lewis, The Lion, the Witch, and the Wardrobe

"American Idol isn't the real world. In the real world, good things come at a cost."

Prayer

If the battery on your iPod runs out of juice, what happens?
No music, right?

What if your car runs out of gas? What happens then?
No driving.

Now, how about if you try to practice courageous generosity
without prayer?

The same thing happens: Your efforts, sooner or later, fall
flat. You can't keep giving. You give the wrong things in the
wrong way. And whatever you do give, you give with the wrong
attitude.

Prayer is the fuel upon which courageous generosity depends.
It's what connects you to God and what gives you the will and
the strength to give until it hurts. It's the means by which you
build a relationship with God.

To build that relationship, the Bible says you need to "continue steadfastly in prayer" (Col 4:2). That means praying just
one day a week won't cut it. Rather, God wants you to turn to
Him repeatedly day in and day out—asking for help when you
need it, thanking Him when help comes, sharing with Him
your thoughts and concerns, saying you're sorry when you've
messed up, and telling Him you love Him over and over again.

It's important to realize that God doesn't want you to pray

like that because He needs it. He wants it because you need it. You need to go to Him constantly, repeatedly, again and again so you can learn to hear His voice speaking to you and see His hand guiding you. You need to go to Him so that you can be transformed by Him and receive the grace you need to live the life He calls you to lead. You need to go to Him so that you can find the strength to love as He loves—with courageous generosity.

Read

1. According to the Catechism (2559 and 2565), what is prayer? What is the foundation of prayer?

_____

_____

_____

2. What does God promise to the humble in 2 Chronicles 7:14–15?

_____

_____

3. What does James 5:13–16 say about the connection between prayer and faith?

_____

_____

4. Read David's prayer in Psalms 62:5–8. How does his prayer reflect the connection between prayer, faith, and humility?

_____

_____

5. In Matthew 21:22, what does Jesus say are the effects of prayers offered in faith?

_____

_____

_____

6. According to the Bible, there are five different forms or types of prayer. Read the following verses, then describe in your own words the form of prayer each verse talks about.

Scripture Verse	Prayer
Luke 2:25–32	
Psalms 13:1–5	
1 John 1:8–10	
Philippians 4:6–7	
Numbers 14:13–20	
Colossians 4:12	
1 Thessalonians 5:18	
Psalms 118:1	
Revelation 5:11–14	
Psalms 98	

7. Read Luke 10:38–41 and answer the following questions:

a) What was Mary's priority?

_____

_____

_____

_____

b) What were Martha's priorities?

_____

_____

c) What was wrong with Martha's priorities?

_____

_____

Reflect

1. Why do you think humility is the foundation of prayer? Describe your own attitude when you go to God in prayer. How do you think developing a spirit of humility could change your prayers and your relationship with God?

_____

_____

_____

2. Sometimes the hardest part of praying is simply getting in the habit of doing it. So many temptations work to keep you from praying as often as you should. What are some of the temptations that get in the way of your prayer life? What are some things you can do to overcome those temptations?

_____

_____

_____

_____

_____

3. Think back to the story about Martha and Mary. Do you ever find yourself acting more like Martha than Mary? Give an example. How can you apply the lesson Jesus taught Martha to your own life?

_____

_____

_____

4. Even when we choose not to pray, it's never because we lack a reason to pray. There are always reasons. Think about the five different forms of prayer you described above. Write down each one below. Next to each one, write a reason you've had this week to pray that kind of prayer. In other words, what happened this week that has given you a reason to praise God, to ask for his help, to give thanks, etc.

a) _____

_____

b) _____

_____

c) _____

_____

d) _____

_____

e) _____

_____

5. Can you think of a time when you tried to practice courageous generosity without relying on God's help? Describe the situation. What were the results? Looking back, how would you do things differently if you could?

_____

_____

_____

6. One of the reasons it can be hard to pray as often as you should is busyness. There are so many things to do that simply finding the time can be hard. Can you think of two or three ways that you can make time for prayer despite your busy schedule? Describe what you can do.

_____

_____

Respond

1. Pray constantly . . . by making the Sign of the Cross whenever you walk or drive past a Catholic Church. Think of it as saying "hi" to Jesus.

2. Pray constantly . . . by keeping a prayer journal. In it, write letters to God about your hopes, your fears, and your desires. Try to spend at least ten minutes every other day writing in the journal.

3. Pray constantly . . . by checking in with God at the beginning and end of each day. Every morning, say a quick prayer of thanks to God for the day and ask for His help to do His will throughout the day. Every night, thank God for getting you through the day, tell Him you're sorry for any mistakes you've made, and ask for His help to do better tomorrow.

MEMORY VERSE

"Have no anxiety about anything, but in everything
by prayer and supplication with thanksgiving
let your requests be made known to God.
And the peace of God, which passes all understanding,
will keep your hearts and your minds in Christ Jesus."
Philippians 4:6–7

A SPIRITUAL BATTLE

Think prayer is easy? Then you had better check your Catechism. It says:

> Prayer is both a gift of grace and a determined response on our part. It always presupposes effort. The great figures of prayer of the Old Covenant before Christ, as well as the Mother of God, the saints, and he himself, all teach us this: Prayer is a battle. Against whom? Against ourselves and against the wiles of the tempter who does all he can to turn man away from prayer, away from union with God. . . . The "spiritual battle" of the Christian's new life is inseparable from the battle of prayer. (2725)

MAKE SPACE FOR GOD

Finding time to pray doesn't have to be hard. Look for it in the small, quiet moments of your day: when you wake up in the morning or go to bed at night; when you're driving in the car or walking to school; when you're standing in line at a store or waiting on hold during a phone call. Use those moments to stay connected with God.

It also helps to give God a little space in your room, a quiet corner where the two of you can talk. It doesn't have to be elaborate, and you can do this even if you share a room. Simply hang up a picture of Jesus or a crucifix, or keep those things on a shelf along with a statue of Mary. The presence of those little items will help remind you to pray and give you a way to focus your mind on God when you do pray.

> "Souls without prayer are like people whose bodies or limbs are paralyzed: they possess feet and hands, but they cannot control them."
>
> St. Teresa of Avila, *Interior Castle*

"Praying just once a week won't cut it. Rather, God wants you to turn to Him repeatedly, day in and day out."

Vocation: The Call to Total Self-Gift

God is calling you to give everything to Him—your heart, your mind, your trust, your hopes, your fears, everything. But doing that takes practice. It's not easy to place everything you have and are in God's hands. You need to work at it. And the way you work at it is through your vocation.

Your vocation is the path God has designed for you to get to Him. On that path, you will find all the challenges, rewards, and grace you need to learn how to give yourself completely to God. You can, of course, choose not to take that path. God doesn't force anything on anyone. He leaves the ultimate decision about where you go up to you. But the path to which He calls you, no matter how challenging it may seem, is always the easiest and most direct route to Him. Other routes might get you there, but they are never as sure and never as simple.

So, what are the paths to which God might call you?

Consecrated life and married life.

Unlike married life, which can only consist of the union between one man and one woman, consecrated life can take many forms. God might call you to be a religious sister, who is active in the world. He might call you to be a contemplative nun, someone who prays for the world behind convent walls. Or He might call you to consecrate yourself to Him as a single woman, someone who works in the world but dedicates herself completely, totally, and permanently to His service.

Both vocations require courageous generosity. It takes courageous generosity to live those calls—to faithfully carry out the responsibilities associated with each. It takes courageous generosity to answer God's call—to choose His path, not your own. And it takes courageous generosity to hear those calls—to empty yourself of the selfishness and self-will that can prevent you from being open to what God has to say.

Read

CONSECRATED LIFE

1.   Read the Catechism 915–918. What is the mission of consecrated life?

_____

_____

_____

2. According to 1 Corinthians 7:32–35, what advantage is there to the consecrated life?

_____

_____

_____

3. Although all Christians are called to image Christ, consecrated people image Him in a special way. Read the passages in the chart below and describe what each tells us about the way Jesus lived His life. Then, describe how consecrated women live in imitation of Jesus.

Scripture Passage	How Jesus Lived	How Consecrated Women Imitate Jesus
John 10:30		
John 14:11		
John 17:7		
2 Corinthians 8:9		
John 4:34		
Philippians 2:8		

4. Consecrated women show Christ to the world in a special way. But they also show the world important truths about how all men and women will one day live in heaven. Read the following passages and describe how they do that.

a) Matthew 22:30 _____

_____

b) Revelation 5:11–12 _____

_____

5. Why does it take courageous generosity to answer a call to consecrated life? Why would anyone choose this way of life? What are the rewards? (See Matthew 25:1–10; Luke 18:28–30; and Song of Solomon 3:1–4.)

_____

_____

_____

MARRIED LIFE

1. Read the Catechism 1604–1605. What is the mission of married love?

_____

_____

_____

2. Genesis 1:26 says that God made man and woman in His image and likeness. How does the vocation of marriage reflect that?

_____

_____

_____

3. What reason does Genesis 2:18–25 give us for the original purpose of marriage?

_____

_____

_____

4. In Genesis 1:28, what does God command man and woman to do? What other purpose of marriage does this command reveal?

_____

_____

_____

5. According to Ephesians 5:22–33, what other relationship does the marriage of a man and a woman image? How are

husbands and wives supposed to love each other? How does marriage help people grow in holiness?

_____

_____

_____

_____

Reflect

1. To what vocation do you believe God may be calling you? Why do you believe that?

_____

_____

2. Have you ever prayed about whether or not you have a vocation to the consecrated life? Why or why not? Does the thought of giving your life to God in that way scare you? If so, why? If not, how does it make you feel?

_____

_____

3. What do you think would be the most challenging aspects of religious life? What do you think would be the most challenging aspects of married life? How could those different challenges help you on the path to holiness?

_____

_____

_____

_____

4. Describe your parents' marriage. What aspects do you want to imitate in your marriage if that's your vocation? What aspects do you not want to imitate? How has your parents' marriage affected your own understanding of marriage? How do you think that might affect you pursuing the vocation of marriage someday?

_____

_____

_____

_____

5. Why do you think answering a call to the consecrated life requires courageous generosity? Why do you think answering a call to married life requires courageous generosity?

_____

_____

_____

_____

6. What are some things you can do now to start discerning your vocation and preparing yourself to answer God's call? Be specific.

_____

_____

Respond

1. Pray for vocations to consecrated life. Ask God to help people hear and answer His call to serve.

2. Pray for vocations to the married life. Ask God to bless,

strengthen, and protect Christian marriages. Especially pray for the marriages of people you know and love.

3. Pray about your own vocation. Ask God to help you hear and answer His call. Spend time talking with married people and consecrated women about their vocations. Visit a convent. And ask God again and again to show you His plan.

MEMORY VERSE

"Then Jesus told his disciples,
'If any man would come after me,
let him deny himself and take up
his cross and follow me.'"
Matthew 16:24

MORE THAN HUMAN

In our culture, marriage is under attack. Divorce is widespread. The push for same-sex marriage is on the rise. And more and more couples choose to live together before marrying. At the heart of all these problems is a fundamental misunderstanding of marriage.

People think of marriage primarily as an intimate relationship with another person, as a way of saying to the world, "I love this person more than anyone else." But that's not what marriage is.

Marriage is a sacrament, a sign of the life-giving union between Christ and His Church. In marriage, the two halves of humanity, male and female, are united by an unbreakable bond. Together they reflect the whole of humanity and the life of the Trinity. Together they also form the foundation for a healthy, holy, happy culture.

That's what marriage is and does. That's how God made it to be. No law can change that. But bad laws that don't respect God's intentions for marriage—plus the relationships of individuals that don't respect God's intentions for marriage—make it much harder for good marriages to exist and flourish. That's why protecting marriage—both through our laws and actions—has to be a top priority for Christians. When marriage suffers, we all suffer.

GET READY

What can you do now that will help you hear, answer, and live God's call? Regardless of whether that call is to consecrated life or married life, these acts of courageous generosity will pave the way for a happier vocation.

Give Jesus your heart, your love, and your time by praying, receiving the Eucharist, and going to Confession as often as possible.

Give Jesus your body, by vowing to remain chaste until marriage.

Study the Scriptures. They are love letters from God to you.

Spend time praying before the Blessed Sacrament, asking the Holy Spirit to show you your struggles and help you overcome them.

In Confession, give over to God every sin and secret keeping you from being who He created you to be. The sins and secrets you keep to yourself will become walls between you and God, and prevent you from hearing God's voice and knowing the desires of your heart.

"Nothing is really lost by a life of sacrifice; everything is lost by failure to obey God's call."

Henry P. Liddon

"The path God calls you too, no matter how challenging it may seem, is always the easiest and most direct route to him. Other routes might get you there, but they are never as sure and never as simple."

The Home Front: Practicing Courageous Generosity with Parents and Siblings

Someday, God could call you to serve Him in the slums of Calcutta or the jungles of Ecuador. He might ask you to feed the hungry in Africa or build shelters for the homeless in Mexico. He could task you with caring for the sick, comforting orphans, or holding the hands of the dying.

But today, Calcutta isn't on the agenda. What is on the agenda is home.

Today, your home, wherever it may be, is your Calcutta. Until the day comes when God calls you elsewhere, it's the primary place where God wants you to live out courageous generosity. And the people with whom you live—your parents, grandparents, or siblings—are the primary people He wants you to serve.

Yes, practicing courageous generosity in your home is far less exciting than practicing it in the deserts of the Sudan or the streets of China. And yes, lending your favorite sweater to your little sister seems to pale in comparison to risking your life in the malaria-infested jungles of Nicaragua. But, more often than not, lending that sweater to your sister is a lot harder than hanging out in malaria-invested jungles. And practicing courageous generosity at home (when no one is looking, and there's not an ounce of drama or adventure) can be much more challenging than practicing it in the Sudan.

The greatest challenge you'll face in your life won't be serving strangers. It will be serving your family, the people who can love you like no one else, hurt you like no one else, and drive you crazy like no one else.

So, how can you meet the challenge?

SIBLINGS

Read

1. From the very beginning, siblings have struggled to get along. Read the following passages. Describe the way in which the siblings written about fail to love each other. What sin is at the heart of all of the conflicts described?

a) Genesis 4:2–10 _____

_____

b) Genesis 27:30–41 _____

_____

c) Genesis 37 _____

_____

2. In Luke 10:38–42, why is Martha frustrated with her sister? Who is in the right in this particular situation? Why?

_____

_____

_____

3. Not all the siblings in the Bible fought with each other. Read the following passages, and describe how the sisters and brothers in each story show their love for one another.

a) Exodus 2:1–8 _____

_____

_____

b) John 1:35–42 _____

_____

_____

c) John 11:1–3; 11:17–28 _____

_____

_____

4. According to Proverbs 17:17, what is one of the reasons why God has given us brothers (and sisters)?

_____

_____

Reflect

1. Have you ever envied one of your siblings or has one of your siblings ever envied you? Describe the situation. What were the consequences? What do you think was the real source of the problem? In other words, what were you (or they) lacking that led to envy?

_____

_____

2. Think back to the story about Martha and Mary. Which sister are you more like? Are you the one who works and gets frustrated when no one else is helping or the one who doesn't work when other people are? What are the strengths and weaknesses in each type of person?

_____

_____

_____

3. Why does it require courageous generosity not to envy your siblings and not to get frustrated with them when they're not doing what you want them to do?

_____

_____

4. Describe some of the ways in which you're generous with your siblings on a daily basis. Is being generous in those ways hard or easy? Why? How has your generosity made a difference in your siblings' lives and in your relationship with them?

_____

_____

_____

5. Describe some of the ways in which you've failed to be generous to your siblings? Why did you fail? How did your failure affect others? What are two ways you can be more generous to them on a daily basis?

_____

_____

PARENTS

Read

1. The fourth commandment is the only one of the Ten Commandments that promises a blessing to those who obey it. Read Exodus 20:12. What is the fourth commandment? What is the blessing attached to it?

_____

_____

_____

2. What do Luke 2:51–52 and John 2:1–11 tell us about the ways in which Jesus obeyed the fourth commandment?

_____

_____

_____

3. Honoring your father and mother requires more than obedience. Read Ruth 1:3–18; 2:18; and 4:13–17. How does Ruth honor the only mother she has, her mother-in-law, Naomi?

_____

_____

_____

4. According to Colossians 3:20, why should you obey your parents?

_____

_____

5. What does 1 Timothy 5:4 call a "religious duty"?

_____

_____

6. Read Sirach 3:1–16. What are the blessings to be gained from honoring your father and mother? In what specific ways does the passage say you should honor them?

_____

_____

_____

Reflect

1. Think of a time when you disobeyed your mom or dad. Describe the situation. What were the consequences? Did you regret being disobedient? Why or why not? What have you learn from that situation?

_____

_____

_____

2. What do you think it means to "honor your father and mother"? What are some of the ways you try to do that on a daily basis? What are two or three additional things you could make a habit of doing that would honor them?

_____

_____

_____

_____

3. Why does it require courageous generosity to honor and obey your parents?

_____

_____

Respond

1. Be generous with prayer. Like Mary and Martha, go to Jesus and ask Him to help your siblings (and your parents).

2. Be generous with time. Invite your siblings to do things with you and your friends, and once in a while pass up time with your friends to spend time at home talking with your mom and dad about their life and yours.

3. Be generous with gratitude. As often as possible, praise your brothers and sisters for what they do right and thank your parents for all that they give and do for you.

MEMORY VERSE

"Honor your father and your mother,
that your days may be long in the land which
the Lord your God gives you."
Exodus 20:12

BROKEN RECORD?

Sometimes the Bible can sound like a broken record. Consider the command to obey your parents. God hands down that instruction no less than a dozen times in both the Old and New Testaments. In the New Testament, if the subject of children and parents comes up, you can pretty much bet the command of obedience comes up too (see Rom 29:30; Col 3:20; 1 Tim 5:4; 2 Tim 3:2). What gives with all the repetition?

Well, if man had never fallen, obeying your parents would be the most natural thing in the world. But ever since men and women rebelled against their heavenly Father, they've been rebelling against their earthly fathers (and mothers) as well. Your parents are a human symbol of your heavenly Father, and finding your way back to obeying Him requires learning to obey the people who represent Him on earth.

That's not always easy, but it is always important. It is, in fact, eternally important. Which is why God tells us to do it so many times. More than just staying out of trouble and getting your allowance depends on it.

NO THIEVING ALLOWED

Proverbs 28:24 says, "He who robs his father or mother and says, 'That is no transgression,' is the companion of a man who destroys."

That's a fairly easy sin to avoid, right? One that you would never even dream of committing?

Maybe. But maybe not.

It might never cross your mind to dip into your dad's wallet or take valuables from your mom's jewelry box, but there are other ways to rob your parents, ways that can hurt you, hurt your relationship with your mom and dad, and undermine all your efforts to practice courageous generosity in other areas.

Those ways could include . . .

. . . Not treating the things that your parents have bought you with respect;

. . . Not treating your parents' things with respect;

. . . Being wasteful of the food they've bought for you or the money they've given to you;

. . . Not working hard in school and squandering the educational opportunities for which their money has paid;

. . . Driving recklessly, endangering both yourself and the car you're driving.

"The great danger for family life, in the midst of any society whose idols are pleasure, comfort and independence, lies in the fact that people close their hearts and become selfish."

Pope John Paul II

"Today, your home, wherever it may be, is your Calcutta. . . . It's the primary place where God wants you to live out courageous generosity."

Love Thy Neighbor

Courageous generosity starts at home. But it doesn't end there. It also doesn't end with your friends or classmates.

God wants you to take responsibility for more than your little corner of the world or circle of friends. And He wants you to think about more than yourself, more than your family, and more than the kids at your school.

God's call to give until it hurts extends to the way you treat your teachers, the way you treat the person in line at the store, the way you treat the homeless person you pass by every day on your way out of church, the way you treat random strangers living in your town, and even the way you treat people whom you'll never meet at all—people who live on the other side of the country or the other side of the world.

Why does God ask so much? Why does He expect so much? And how on earth does He expect you to care for people you never even meet?

Let's find out.

Read

1. According to Matthew 22:35–40, what are the two greatest commandments?

_____

_____

2. In the passage cited above, Jesus says the second greatest commandment is "like" the greatest. How are they similar?

_____

_____

_____

3. According to the following passages, what are we doing when we love one another?

a) Romans 13:8–10 _____

_____

b) Galatians 5:13–14 _____

_____

4. Read John 15:12–14. According to Jesus, how do we love our neighbor? What does that mean?

_____

_____

5. Read Luke 1:36–40 and describe the conditions under which Mary makes her visit to her cousin Elizabeth. What does this

story tell us about loving our neighbor?

_____

_____

_____

6. In John 2:1–11, Mary again shows us what it means to love our neighbors. Describe what she does. How would she have noticed the couple was low on wine? Why did she ask her son to help?

_____

_____

_____

7. Matthew 18:21–22 and Matthew 7:1–5 describe two common obstacles that can prevent you from loving your neighbor. What are they? How does Jesus say you are to respond to those obstacles?

_____

_____

_____

_____

8. Ephesians 4:25–32 gives several practical steps you can take to love your neighbors as Jesus wants you to. List some of those steps.

_____

_____

_____

Reflect

1. In John 4:3–26, Jesus is tired and worn out from helping people, and just when he sits down to rest, a stranger—a Samaritan woman—appears and is in need of his help. Despite how tired He is, Jesus helps her. Has someone ever approached you for help when you were tired? What was your response? Was it the right one? Why or why not?

_____

_____

_____

2. Have you ever done something to help a stranger—given money to an important cause, volunteered at a soup kitchen, or something similar? If so, describe what you did. Was it hard to give up that time or money? How did you feel afterwards? If not, why haven't you done something to help a stranger and what can you do to change that?

_____

_____

_____

3. Part of loving your neighbor is forgiving your neighbor. Is there anyone you're struggling to forgive? How do you think that makes them feel? Based upon what you've learned in this lesson, how do you think that affects your relationship with God? Describe a situation where someone forgave you and how you felt afterwards. Does that make you want to forgive others? Why or why not?

_____

_____

4. Another part of loving your neighbor is not judging them. Have you ever been judged unfairly? Describe what happened and how that made you feel. Is there someone you might be judging unfairly? Who? Why do you think you're doing that? How does judging someone get in the way of you loving them and God as you should?

_____

_____

_____

_____

5. What are some practical things you can do to be more loving towards your friends and classmates? Your teachers? Strangers?

_____

_____

_____

Respond

1. Talk to your neighbor. Make a point of talking with people you don't know in school or your neighborhood, especially people who might not have anyone else to talk to.

2. Learn about your neighbor. When you're talking with someone, don't just talk about yourself. Ask people about their hopes, their fears, and their beliefs. Seek to understand them as you want to be understood.

3. Read about your neighbor. You can't love the neighbors you've never seen if you don't know anything about them. So start reading a major newspaper or website at least once a week to learn about all the people who need your love around the world.

MEMORY VERSE

"So faith by itself, if it has
no works, is dead."
James 2:17

AN INSTRUMENT OF YOUR PEACE

Looking for a prayer to help you love your neighbor as you should? Try praying the Prayer of St. Francis of Assisi every day. Put a copy on your bedroom mirror. Memorize it if you can. And most important, try to live that for which you're asking.

Prayer of Saint Francis of Assisi

Lord, make me an instrument of your peace.
Where there is hatred, let me sow love;
where there is injury, pardon;
where there is doubt, faith;
where there is despair, hope;
where there is darkness, light;
and where there is sadness, joy.

O Divine Master, grant that I may not so much seek
to be consoled as to console;
to be understood as to understand;
to be loved as to love.
For it is in giving that we receive;
it is in pardoning that we are pardoned;
and it is in dying that we are born to eternal life. Amen.

MODELING MARY

In the stories you've read about Mary in this lesson, she did three things that teach us how to love our neighbor. First, she noticed that there was a need. This required paying attention to those around her, listening to them, and seeing even the needs that went unspoken. It meant taking notice of people and needs beyond her own and those of her immediate circle.

Secondly, Mary stepped out of her comfort zone. It wasn't easy for Mary to travel all that way to care for Elizabeth or to risk that others might think she was intruding in another's wedding. She risked that people might think badly of her or think her a little odd. But she knew the risk was worth the reward of helping others.

Finally, she did something to remedy the need. She went on the journey. She got Jesus to turn water into wine. She didn't wait for someone else to do it. She took action. And she did this without complaining, judging, or gossiping.

Essentially, Mary died to herself. She was more interested in others, more interested in serving and helping them, than she was interested in herself. And that is what courageous generosity is all about.

"*Stretch out your hand often by doing favors for your neighbor, by protecting from harm one who suffers under the weight of calumny; stretch out your hand to the poor man who begs from you; stretch out your hand to the Lord asking pardon for your sins. This is how you stretch out your hand, and this is how you will be cured.*"

St. Ambrose of Milan

"God wants you to take responsibility for more than your little
corner of the world or circle of
friends. And he wants you to
think about more than yourself,
more than your family, and more
than the kids at your school."

Work & Money

Contrary to popular opinion, life is not about what you get. It's about what you give. In the end, "whoever has the most toys," does not win. There's no prize for greed, just as there's no applause for laziness. Both of those attitudes are celebrated by our culture. But both are spiritually toxic.

If you want to become a saint, you have to let go of dreams of fame and fortune, lounging with ease in Beverly Hills mansions, and obtaining celebrity in American Idol fashion—instantly and overnight. Becoming a saint is a way better gig than becoming the next American Idol, but it also requires a whole different attitude towards the way you spend your time. It requires a different attitude towards work.

Basically, if you want to be a saint, you have to go to work for God. That doesn't necessarily mean becoming a priest or a nun or teaching religion at a Catholic school. It means doing whatever job He has called you to do—including your studies—for his glory. It means giving your all to serving Him by serving others. It means working with honesty, integrity, and passion. Work is not punishment: It's a path to sainthood, a path that teaches you virtues as it helps you grow in grace.

Work also gives you the opportunity to serve others not just by what you do but also with what you earn. Work allows you to practice good stewardship, wisely spending and giving away the fruit of your labors (i.e., money).

Again, life is not about what you get. It's about what you give. It's about how well you live courageous generosity. And both how and why you work, as well as what you do with what you earn through your work, go into determining whether you get the prize at the end of the journey: sainthood.

WORK

Read

1. What instructions does God give to man in Genesis 1:28 and Genesis 2:15?

_____

_____

_____

2. When are those instructions given to Adam and Eve—before or after they fell from grace? What does that timing tell us about the place of work in God's plan?

_____

_____

_____

3. According to Genesis 3:17–19, how does God's plan for work change after the Fall?

_____

_____

_____

4. Read 1 Corinthians 12. How is the Body of Christ affected by its members' different gifts and talents?

_____

_____

_____

5. Read the following passages, and in your own words describe what each has to say about the value of work.

a) Proverbs 12:24 _____

_____

_____

b) Sirach 19:1 _____

_____

_____

c) Colossians 3:23–24_____

_____

_____

6. Right now, even though you're not getting paid for it, you still have a full-time job: being a student. How well you do that job will determine how well you're able to do the job that God has for you in the future. What other reasons do the following proverbs give you for working hard at your job as a student?

a) Proverbs 1:7 _____

_____

_____

b) Proverbs 8:11 _____

_____

_____

c) Proverbs 16:22 _____

_____

_____

Reflect

1. When you're working either at your studies, a part-time job, or even just helping out around the house, what tasks do you find the most difficult? How do you deal with those difficulties? Do you complain, try to find ways to get out of the job, or do you offer the challenges up to Christ? How can you respond to the challenges of difficult work better in the future?

_____

_____

_____

2. God has given you a lot of special gifts and talents. What are some of those gifts? How could you use those gifts and talents one day to serve others and God? What are you doing now to develop those talents?

_____

_____

_____

3. Have you ever thought of being a student as your job? How does thinking of school that way change your attitude towards

it? What are things you can do on a regular basis to do that job better? Why do you think doing better at this job matters?

_____

_____

MONEY

Read

1. According to Ephesians 4:28 and 2 Thessalonians 3:8–12, what is the good that comes of earning money?

_____

_____

2. What does Psalms 37:21 say about what it means to be a good steward of money?

_____

_____

3. 1 Timothy 6:10 warns against the love of money. Why?

_____

_____

4. According to the following passages, where are many people tempted to place their trust? Where should you place it instead? Why?

a) Hebrews 13:5 _____

_____

b) Proverbs 11:28 _____

_____

c) 1 Timothy 6:17 _____

_____

d) Luke 12:22–34 _____

_____

5. In Luke 12:33, Jesus instructs us to "give alms," which is another way of saying we should give money to those in need. God promises that if you're generous with your money, He'll be generous with you. Read the following passages and list the blessings God promises to those who are generous with money.

a) Tobit 4:7 _____

_____

b) Tobit 12:8–9 _____

_____

c) Sirach 3:30 _____

_____

d) Sirach 35:2 _____

_____

e) Sirach 40:24 _____

_____

6. Not all almsgiving is necessarily good. In Matthew 23:23, what is wrong with the offering the Pharisees make? According to Matthew 6:2–4, what should be your attitude when you give something away?

_____

_____

_____

Reflect

1. What is the culture's attitude towards money? Based upon what you've learned in this study, what is wrong with that attitude?

_____

_____

_____

2. Can you think of some examples of what "love of money" looks like in our culture today?

_____

_____

3. Think about your own spending habits. How much money do you have to spend in a given month? What do you spend it on? Do you give away any of the money you earn (or that your parents give you)? Why or why not? What are some good causes

to which you could make a donation? How do you think giving a certain percentage away every month would change your attitude towards money?

_____

_____

_____

_____

_____

Respond

1. Develop the mind God has given you. Commit at least thirty minutes a day to reading a book or newspaper. Reading is the best way to sharpen your intellect and give you wisdom about the world around you.

2. Offer it up. The next time your teacher assigns a really difficult homework assignment or your mom asks you to do a really unpleasant chore, don't complain. Just accept the job and see it as an opportunity to grow in virtue.

3. Start an alms fund. Save a percentage of your allowance or paycheck every month and give it to a charity that you believe in.

MEMORY VERSE

"If then you have not been faithful
with unrighteous mammon [money],
who will entrust to you
the true riches?"
Luke 16:11

WHAT THE CATECHISM SAYS . . . ON WORK

Human work proceeds directly from persons created in the image of God and called to prolong the work of creation by subduing the earth, both with and for one another [Cf. Gen 1:28; GS 34; CA 31]. Hence work is a duty. . . . Work honors the Creator's gifts and the talents received from him. It can also be redemptive. By enduring the hardship of work [Cf. Gen 3:14–19] in union with Jesus, the carpenter of Nazareth and the one crucified on Calvary, man collaborates in a certain fashion with the Son of God in his redemptive work. He shows himself to be a disciple of Christ by carrying the cross, daily, in the work he is called to accomplish [Cf. LE 27]. Work can be a means of sanctification and a way of animating earthly realities with the Spirit of Christ.

Catechism of the Catholic Church 2427

WHAT THE CATECHISM SAYS . . . ON MONEY

A theory that makes profit the exclusive norm and ultimate end of economic activity is morally unacceptable. The disordered desire for money cannot but produce perverse effects. It is one of the causes of the many conflicts which disturb the social order [Cf. GS 63 § 3; LE 7; 20; CA 35].

A system that 'subordinates the basic rights of individuals and of groups to the collective organization of production' is contrary to human dignity [GS 65 § 2]. Every practice that reduces persons to nothing more than a means of profit enslaves man, leads to idolizing money, and contributes to the spread of atheism.

Catechism of the Catholic Church 2424

"You must understand now more clearly that God is calling you to serve Him 'in and from' the ordinary, material and secular activities of human life. He waits for us every day, in the laboratory, in the operating theatre, in the army barracks, in the university lecture room, in the factory, in the workshops, in the field, in the home, and in all the immense panorama of work. Understand this well: there is something holy, something divine hidden in the most ordinary situations, and it is up to each one of you to discover it."

St. Josemaria Escriva, Friends of God

"If you want to become a saint, you have to let go of dreams of fame and fortune, lounging with ease in Beverly Hills mansions, and obtaining celebrity in American Idol fashion."

Sharing the Gospel

What do you do when something good happens to you? When the cute boy at school smiles at you? When you get a new iPod? When you find out that your mom is going to have a new baby?

You share the news, right? You tell someone. You post the news on your Facebook page, you text message your best friend, or you Twitter all your followers. You also might tell your friends the old fashioned way: call them on the phone, run down the street to their house, or make an announcement at the lunch table.

However you do it, the point is that you do it. And you do it immediately, with excitement and joy. You don't sit on the good news. You don't keep it to yourself. Part of the fun is getting to tell people, seeing their reaction, and celebrating with them.

What's true about getting a new iPod should be a thousand times more true about the Good News of salvation. Knowing that God loves you, died for you, and is ready to give you every grace you need in order to spend eternity in perpetual bliss is way more exciting than an iPod touch.

And yet, even though the Good News about Christ is the best news anyone could ever possibly get, it's sometimes the hardest to share.

After all, your friends understand why a new iPod is cool. But they might, at least at first, have a hard time understanding why Jesus' love is even cooler. They might be excited to hear it. But they also might look at you funny, laugh at you, or simply walk away.

But no matter how they react to the Good News, your friends still need to hear it. Everyone needs to hear it. They need it. They can't live without it. And whether they realize it at first or not, they want it. Knowing and loving God is what they were made for.

So how do you start sharing the Good News?

With courageous generosity.

Read

1. What was the last command Jesus gave to His disciples before He ascended into heaven in Matthew 28:18–20?

_____

_____

2. During His life on earth, Jesus set the example for how you are to share the Gospel with others. Using the following Bible passages, complete the table below.

Passage	Who is Jesus helping?	What is their position in society?	Who is a modern parallel?	What is Jesus' message?
John 3:1-15				
John 4:6-26				
John 17:37-44				

Matthew 9:9-13				

3. There's not only one right way to talk with people about Jesus. Jesus Himself used lots of different ways. Read the following passages. After each, describe how Jesus communicated the truth about Himself to people.

a) Matthew 9:27–31 _____

_____

b) Matthew 14:13–21 _____

_____

c) Luke 5:1–11 _____

_____

d) Luke 4:16–22 _____

_____

e) Luke 19:1–8 _____

_____

4. According to Romans 10:14–17; 1 Corinthians 9:16; and 1 Thessalonians 2:2–4, why should you talk with other people about Jesus and your faith?

_____

_____

5. Belief in Christ isn't about what you say. It's about what you do. According to Romans 12:2–21, what should a person's life start to look like after they've heard about Jesus and put their faith in Him?

_____

_____

6. According to Matthew 5:14–17, what should be the role of Christians in the culture? What does this have to do with sharing the Gospel?

_____

_____

_____

7. Read Philippians 4:5–9. What does Paul promise will happen to those who embrace and live the Christian faith?

_____

_____

Reflect

1. Think back to the first time you really and truly believed with your whole heart that Jesus was the Son of God, that He died to save you, and that He loves you with a love deeper than you can imagine. How did you come to believe that? Who were the people that helped you believe that? What made their witness to you so effective?

_____

_____

_____

2. What lessons can you draw from your own conversion experience that can help you share the Good News with others?

_____

_____

3. Are there any areas of your life where you have shut the door to the Gospel? Areas where you are not willing to be converted? If so, how do you think this compromises your ability to share the Gospel with others?

_____

_____

_____

4. Have you ever hesitated to talk with your friends about Jesus and the Church or to speak up about what you believe is right? If so, describe the situation. Why did you keep silent? What would you do differently if you had the chance?

_____

_____

_____

5. Think back to the different ways Jesus taught people about Himself. Besides being the Son of God, what are some of the things that helped Him preach the Gospel so effectively? What can you learn from His example? What are some of the ways you can imitate Him?

_____

_____

_____

6. Think about all the gifts God has given you. Which of those gifts can help you share the Good News with people? What are some of the ways you can use those gifts to help people know Christ and His Church? Are you using any of those gifts now? If so, how?

_____

_____

_____

_____

Respond

1. Know your faith better. Spend one hour on your own each week learning more about what the Catholic Church teaches so that you know what you're talking about when you go to share the Gospel.

2. Have a talk with the Holy Spirit. Before you go into situations where you may be called upon to defend the faith or share the Gospel with others, say a quick prayer to the Holy Spirit asking for His help.

3. Evangelize with your wardrobe. Look for T-shirts, medals, or bags that make a statement about your faith and wear them to school or out with your friends. You'll be evangelizing without words, and maybe even inspire someone to ask a question about what you believe.

MEMORY VERSE

"And he said to them, 'Go into
all the world and preach the
gospel to the whole creation.'"
Mark 16:15

JUST THE FACTS, MA'AM

Do you want to share the faith but feel like you don't know enough to teach others? Then go back to school. Online you'll find tons of great websites that can answer any questions you might have and any questions that others might ask you. Check out these websites for the facts about the faith.

LifeTeen.com

PhatMass.com

Chastity.com

CatholicAnswers.com

Cuf.org

COME HOLY SPIRIT

Before Jesus sent out the Twelve Apostles to preach the Good News to the whole world, He first sent them the Holy Spirit. The Holy Spirit's job was to give them understanding, guide them in difficult situations, and help them find the right words and actions when they were called upon to share the Gospel.

Two thousand years later, the Holy Spirit's job remains the same. The next time you're called upon to talk with others about Jesus, ask for His help. Here's a short prayer that can help you do that.

Come Holy Spirit, fill the hearts of your faithful
and enkindle in them the fire of your love.
Send forth your Spirit and they shall be created.
And You shall renew the face of the earth.
O, God, who by the light of the Holy Spirit,
did instruct the hearts of the faithful,

grant that by the same Holy Spirit
we may be truly wise and ever enjoy His consolations,
Through Christ Our Lord,
Amen.

"Preach the Gospel always. When necessary, use words."

Attributed to St. Francis of Assisi

"Knowing that God loves you, died for you, and is ready to give you every grace you need in order to spend eternity in perpetual bliss is way more exciting than an iPod touch."

Lesson 1: *Courageous Generosity*

COURAGE

READ

1. **A:** Joshua was to lead the Israelites into the Promised Land and reclaim it for the Israelites. This was a dangerous and daunting task. They were going into battle with the odds against them. The land was inhabited by a race of fierce warriors, and they would face a well-armed and well-fortified enemy.

2. **A:** "I will not fail you or forsake you."

3. **A:** Pharaoh's army advances on the Israelites, and they are terrified. They tell Moses that it would have been better to remain slaves in Egypt than to die in the desert. Their fear causes them to say that.

4. **A:** Judas betrayed Him, and the other Apostles fled and denied Christ in His hour of need. They were afraid.

5. **A:** God loves us enough to have even the hairs of our head numbered. He is intimately involved in our lives. He is a loving Father, and with Him in control, we have nothing to fear.

6. **A:** We have received a spirit of sonship. We are children of God and therefore should be free from the slavery of sin and fear.

REFLECT

1–3. **A:** Answers will vary as they will reflect your own thoughts and experiences.

GENEROSITY

READ

1. **A: a–d)** We are to give freely and abundantly of our time, our energy, our prayers, and our love; practice patience; endure

sufferings; imitate Christ. They all require self-sacrifice, dying to self, and putting on Christ.

2. **A:** You will be enriched and blessed. You will get back what you give.

3. **A:** Answers will vary but can include: God became man— His infancy, serving when tired, associating with the outcasts of the world, the Eucharist, suffering for our sins, welcoming the Gentiles into His kingdom, etc.

REFLECT

1–3. **A:** Answers will vary as they will reflect your own thoughts and experiences.

Lesson 2: *Sacrifice: The Way to Joy*

READ

1. **A:** God sacrificed animals from the Garden of Eden. Literally, the sacrifice was made to give Adam and Eve animal skins with which they could cover their nakedness. Figuratively, it covered over their sin. Sacrifices atone for sin.

2. **A:** Thanksgiving. God saved the lives of Noah and his family, and promised to never destroy humanity again with a flood.

3. **A:** a) Sons. b) Abraham is to sacrifice his son Isaac. Hannah must give her son to the Lord. c) He wanted Abraham to be willing to make the sacrifice as a demonstration of his faith in God and his trust in God's promise. d) Hannah was willing because she recognized that her son was a gift from the Lord and that he belonged to God, not her.

4. **A:** God is not pleased with sacrifices when those making them are not righteous and don't practice justice, mercy, or compassion. A pleasing sacrifice is when we offer God the best we have in faith; when our sacrifices are an expression of love, not an attempt to bargain with God; and when the way we live our lives is also an expression of that love.

5. **A:** God required them to make so many sacrifices as a way of perpetually reminding them of their sinfulness and helping them understand that nothing they alone could do could ever undo the consequences of the Fall.

6. **A:** Christ's offering of Himself on Calvary and the continuation of that offering before God in heaven.

7. **A:** We should continue to make sacrifices in imitation of Christ, as reparation for our sins, to produce character and faith, and to build up the body of Christ. Our sufferings merit grace for those whom we suffer, as well as grace for us. They connect us more intimately to Christ's sufferings in His sacrifice, and they help make up for the suffering of sin.

8. **A:** We are to offer our bodies as a "living sacrifice" to God.

REFLECT

1–6. **A:** Answers will vary as they will reflect your own thoughts and experiences.

Lesson 3: *Prayer*

READ

1. **A:** "Prayer is the raising of one's mind and heart to God or the requesting of good things from God" and "the life of prayer is the habit of being in the presence of the thrice-holy God and in communion with him." Humility is the foundation of prayer.

2. **A:** God hears the prayers of the humble.

3. **A:** When we have faith, we realize that God is concerned with us in both good times and bad. All circumstances are opportunities to pray. Furthermore, faith informs us that God is the one who is ultimately in control and prayer is our acknowledgement of this fact.

4. **A:** David expresses humility and complete trust in the Lord. His response to humility and faith is prayer.

5. **A:** We will receive what we ask for.

6. **A:**

Reference Verses	Prayer Form
Luke 2:25-35 Psalms 103:1-5	Blessing & Adoration: (See CCC 2626–2628) These are prayers that acknowledge the wonder and magnificence of God.
1 John 1:8-10 Philippians 4:6-7	Petition: (See CCC 2629–2633) These are our spontaneous requests of God, either for His blessings or forgiveness.
Numbers 14:13-20 Colossians 4:12	Intercession: (See CCC 2634–2636) These are the requests we make for the benefit of others.
1 Thessalonians 5:18 Psalms 118:1	Thanksgiving: (See CCC 2637–2638) These are our prayers of gratitude.
Revelation 5:11-14 Psalms 98	Praise: (See CCC 2639–2643) This is when we acknowledge and honor God for who He is.

7. A: a) Mary's priority was listening to Jesus. b) Martha's priorities were serving the meal and getting the house ready. c) Martha was doing those things at the cost of not paying attention to Jesus.

REFLECT

1–6. A: Answers will vary as they will reflect your own thoughts and experiences.

Lesson 4: *Vocation: The Call to Total Self-Gift*

CONSECRATED LIFE

READ

1. **A:** To follow Christ more nearly through a total gift of self, to serve the kingdom of God, and to be a sign of the glory to come in the kingdom of God, all through living a life of celibacy, poverty, and obedience.

2. **A:** Those who are consecrated are more free to pursue holiness and serve others because they don't have to concern themselves first and foremost with caring for a husband or wife.

3. **A:**

Scripture Passage	How Jesus Lived	How Consecrated Women Imitate Jesus
John 10:30 John 14:11	Christ was one with the Father and lived a life exclusively devoted to serving Him	Consecrated women take a vow of celibacy, promising never to marry, so they can serve Christ above all
John 17:7 2 Corinthians 8:9	Christ lived a life of perfect poverty, owning nothing	Consecrated women take a vow of poverty, promising to live simply and not be caught up in the things of the world
John 4:34 Philippians 2:8	Christ was obedient to the Father in all things	Consecrated women take a vow of obedience, submitting to the Church, their religious order, and their community's superior

4. **A:** a) They live now like all will in heaven—unmarried. b) They devote much of their life to praising and worshipping God, as all do in heaven.

5. **A:** It takes courageous generosity because a great deal has to be given up in order to serve God well in religious life—a husband, physical children, material prosperity, and self-will. The rewards, however, are great. Like the wise virgins, those

who remain faithful to their vows in religious life will receive the same reward. They will get to be with the bridegroom, Christ, in heaven; they will also receive more in heaven than they ever gave up on earth; and they will get to be with Christ, whom they love, for all eternity.

MARRIED LIFE

READ

1. **A:** To image the love of God, to bring children into the world, and to help one another.
2. **A:** God is a family of Three Persons: the Father, Son, and Holy Spirit. Each gives Himself entirely to the other in love. Man and woman are the only creatures capable of giving themselves as a gift to another. They do this in marriage.
3. **A:** It was not good for man to be alone; he needed a helper "fit for him."
4. **A:** Be fruitful and multiply. One of the essential purposes of marriage is to bring children into the world.
5. **A:** The marriage of a man and woman is supposed to image the relationship of Christ and His Church. Husbands and wives are supposed to be subject to one another, submitting to one another and loving each other as Christ loves the Church. Doing that requires dying to oneself, which is essential on the path to holiness.

REFLECT

1–6. **A:** Answers will vary as they will reflect your own thoughts and experiences.

Lesson 5: *The Home Front: Practicing Courageous Generosity with Parents and Siblings*

SIBLINGS

READ

1. **A:** a) Cain murdered his brother Abel because God was more pleased with Abel's sacrifice than with Cain's. b) Esau plots to kill Jacob when he discovers that his younger brother received his father's blessing. c) Joseph's brothers planned to kill him, but then sold him into slavery instead. In each instance, envy was the root cause of the problems between the brothers.

2. **A:** Martha is working hard and grows frustrated with Mary because Mary is listening to Jesus instead of helping Martha. Mary was in the right in this situation because she was doing what Jesus wanted her to do—being with Him.

3. **A:** a) Moses' sister protected him as he journeyed along the Nile in a basket, then made sure he was taken to his mother to be nursed. b) Andrew ran to tell his brother Peter about Jesus and brought Peter to meet Jesus. c) Mary and Martha interceded for their brother, asking Jesus first to heal him, and later, to raise him from the dead.

4. **A:** To help us during the hardest of times.

REFLECT

1–5. **A:** Answers will vary as they will reflect your own thoughts and experiences.

PARENTS

READ

1. **A:** "Your days will be long in the land which the Lord your God gives you."

2. **A:** As a child, Jesus was obedient to His parents. At Cana, Jesus began His public ministry, performing His first miracle at His mother's command.

3. **A:** Ruth stayed with Naomi, refusing to leave her on her

own. She then provided for Naomi, working hard to ensure there was food for the both of them. Ruth then included Naomi in her new life with her new husband and their child.

4. **A:** It pleases God.

5. **A:** To take care of your parents in their old age.

6. **A:** Honoring your father and mother will atone for your sins, earn you long life, store up treasure for you in heaven, help your prayers be heard, and bring you the gift of children. You honor your parents by being patient with them, bearing their faults kindly, obeying them, listening to them, and caring for them.

REFLECT

1–3. **A:** Answers will vary as they will reflect your own thoughts and experiences.

Lesson 6: *Love Thy Neighbor*

READ

1. **A:** To love God with all your heart, soul, mind, and strength, and to love your neighbor as yourself.

2. **A:** We tend to love ourselves more than anyone—with all our heart, soul, mind, and strength. So if we love our neighbor like we love ourselves, we are loving them with all our heart, soul, mind, and strength, which is also how we are called to love God.

3. **A:** a) We are fulfilling the law of God. b) We are being servants to one another.

4. **A:** We are to love one another like Jesus loved us, dying for each other if necessary, as Christ died for us.

5. **A:** Mary was newly pregnant and probably very overwhelmed by what the angel told her, but she still made the long journey up into the hill country to help Elizabeth. This story shows us we must love our neighbor even when the timing is inconvenient or causes difficulty for us.

6. **A:** Mary notices that the couple is running out of wine and takes steps to remedy the situation. In order to notice the problem, Mary wasn't just enjoying herself. She was being attentive to what was going on around her, and probably helping serve in some way. She asked Jesus to help because she knew the couple would be humiliated if they ran out of wine.

7. **A:** Others' sins against us can make it difficult for us to love them as we should, as can their faults. We are supposed to forgive them for what they've done to us, even if that means forgiving again and again. We are also supposed to be more concerned with overcoming our faults than judging others on theirs.

8. **A:** Forgive one another; let go of anger; do kind deeds; give to those in need; don't speak badly about other people; don't be jealous or bitter or seek revenge.

REFLECT

1–3. **A:** Answers will vary as they will reflect your own thoughts and experiences.

Lesson 7: *Work & Money*

WORK

READ

1. **A:** Subdue the earth, have dominion over all the creatures and things living in the world, till the ground, and keep the Garden.
2. **A:** The instructions are given before the Fall, which tells us that work was part of God's plan from the beginning. Man was made to be a creature who works.
3. **A:** Work became hard and difficult, and it wouldn't always bear the fruit it was supposed to bear.
4. **A:** All the gifts work together, so that the members of the Body can help one another and help the Body as a whole.
5. **A:** a) Those who work hard will be rewarded with leadership and success. b) Those who work hard at the small things will be successful. c) Work hard in everything for God and He will reward you.
6. **A:** If we don't seek wisdom and instruction, we will be considered fools; the wisdom we acquire through learning is better than jewels (or money); wisdom will give us life.

REFLECT

1–3. **A:** Answers will vary as they will reflect your own thoughts and experiences.

WORK

READ

1. **A:** So we can give to those in need, so we don't have to take from others, and so we have enough to provide for our needs.
2. **A:** We should never borrow what we cannot repay. Rather, we should generously give our money away and not expect repayment.
3. **A:** The love of money is the root of all evil and leads people away from God.
4. **A:** People are tempted to place their trust in riches, but we

should place our trust in God. If we put our trust in riches, we will wither. But God has promised if we put our trust in Him, He will never forsake us and will give us all we need.

5. **A:** a) If we don't turn away from the poor, God won't turn away from us. b) It will deliver us from death and help us enter into eternal life. c) It will atone for our sins. d) Our alms will be considered Thank offerings to God. e) It will bring us rescue in times of trouble.

6. **A:** They have placed more importance on giving alms than they did on being kind, just, merciful, and charitable. We should keep our almsgiving a secret, not letting others know what we're doing.

REFLECT

1–3. A: Answers will vary as they will reflect your own thoughts and experiences.

Lesson 8: *Sharing the Gospel*

READ

1. **A:** To go and baptize all nations and teach them what Christ commanded.

2. **A:** God hears the prayers of the humble.

3. **A:** a) Healing. b) Feeding. c) Working alongside His disciples. d) Preaching. e) Spending time with people.

4. **A:** a) People can't believe in Christ if they have never heard of Him, and they can only hear about Him if those who know Christ tell them. b) We preach out of necessity. c) God has entrusted us to preach the Gospel.

5. **A:** They shouldn't follow the ways of the world, but rather use their gifts for service to the Body of Christ, practice the virtues, and be charitable.

6. **A:** We are to be a witness in the midst of the world. We need to share the Gospel through our words as much as our actions.

7. **A:** God will give us His peace.

REFLECT

1–6. A: Answers will vary as they will reflect your own thoughts and experiences.